The Arabian Nights

Or,

The Thousand and One Nights

[Christmas Summary Classics]

(Various Authors)

KARTINDO PUBLISHING HOUSE (Kartindo.com)

The Arabian Nights

There is as much doubt about the history of "The Thousand and One Nights" as that which veils the origin of the Homeric poems. It is said that a certain Caliph Shahryar, having been deceived by his wife, slew her, and afterwards married a wife only for one day, slaying her on the morning after. When this slaughter of women had continued some time he became wedded to one Shahrazad, daughter of his Vizir, who, by telling the Commander of the Faithful exciting stories and leaving them unfinished every dawn, so provoked the Caliph's curiosity that he kept her alive, and at last grew so fond of her that he had no thought of putting her to death. As for the authorship of the stories, they are certainly not the work of one mind, and have probably grown with the ages into their present form. The editions published for Christian countries do not represent the true character of these legends, which are often exceedingly sensual. The European versions of this extraordinary entertainment began in 1704 with the work of one Antoine Galland, Professor of Arabic at the College of France, a Frenchman who, according to Sir Richard Burton, possessed "in a high degree that art of telling a tale which is far more captivating than culture or scholarship." Sir R. Burton (see Vol. XIX) summed up what may be definitely believed of the Nights in the following conclusion: The framework of the book is purely Persian perfunctorily Arabised, the archetype being the Hazar Afsanah. The oldest tales may date from the reign of Al-Mansur, in the eighth century; others belong to the tenth century; and the latest may be ascribed to the sixteenth. The work assumed its present form in the thirteenth century. The author is unknown, "for the best reason; there never was one."

KARTINDO PUBLISHING HOUSE (Kartindo.com)

I.--The Seven Voyages of Sindbad the Sailor

When the father of Sindbad was taken to Almighty Allah, much wealth came to the possession of his son; but soon did it dwindle in boon companionship, for the city of Baghdad is sweet to the youthful. Then did Sindbad bethink him how he might restore his fortune, saying to himself: "Three things are better than other three; the day of death is better than the day of birth, a live dog is better than a dead lion, and the grave is better than want"; and gathering merchandise together, he took ship and sailed away to foreign countries.

Now it came to pass that the captain of this ship sighted a strange island, whereon were grass and trees, very pleasant to the eyes. So they anchored, and many went ashore. When these had gathered fruits, they made a fire, and were about to warm themselves, when the captain cried out from the ship: "Ho there! passengers, run for your lives and hasten back to the ship and leave your gear and save yourselves from destruction. Allah preserve you! For this island whereon ye stand is no true island, but a great fish stationary a-middlemost of the sea, whereon the sand hath settled and trees have sprung up of old time, so that it is become like unto an island; but when ye lighted fires on it, it felt the heat and moved; and in a moment it will sink with you into the depths of the sea and ye will be drowned."

When the fish moved, the captain did not wait for his passengers, but sailed away, and Sindbad, seizing a tub, floated helpless in the great waters. But by the mercy of Allah he was thrown upon a true island, where a beautiful mare lay upon the ground, who cried at his approach. Then a man started up at the mare's cry, and seeing Sindbad, bore him to an underground chamber, where he regaled the waif with plenteous food. To him did this man explain how he was a groom of King Mirjan, and that he brought the king's mares to pasture on the island, hiding underground while the stallions of the sea came up out of the waves unto the mares. Presently Sindbad saw this strange sight, and witnessed how the groom drove the stallions back to the waves when they would have dragged the mares with them. After that he was carried before King Mirjan, who entreated him kindly, and when he had amassed wealth, returned by ship to Bussorah, and so to Baghdad.

But becoming possessed with the thought of travelling about the ways of men, he set out on a second voyage. And it came to pass that he landed with others on a lovely island, and lay down to sleep, after he had eaten many delicious fruits. Awaking, he found the ship gone. Then, praying to Almighty Allah, like a man distracted, he roamed about the island, presently climbing a tree to see what he could see. And he saw a great dome afar, and journeyed to it.

There was no entrance to this white dome, and as he went round about it, the sun became suddenly darkened, so that he looked towards it in fear, and lo! a bird in the heavens whose wings blackened all light. Then did Sindbad know that the dome was an egg, and that the bird was the bird roc, which feeds its young upon elephants. Sore afraid, he hid himself, and the bird settled upon the egg, and brooded upon it. Then Sindbad unwound his turban, and, tying one end to the leg of the great bird and the other about his own middle, waited for the dawn.

When the dawn was come, the bird flew into the heavens, unaware of the weight at its foot, and Sindbad was borne across great seas and far countries. When at last the bird settled on land, Sindbad unfastened his turban, and was free.

But the place was filled with frightful serpents, and strewn with diamonds. Sindbad saw a dead sheep on the ground, with diamonds sticking to its carcase, and he knew that this was a device of merchants, for eagles come and carry away these carcases to places beyond the reach of the serpents, and merchants take the diamonds sticking to the flesh. So he hid himself under the carcase, and an eagle bore him with it to inhabited lands, and he was delivered.

Again it came to him to travel, and on this his third voyage the ship was driven to the mountain of Zughb, inhabited by hairy apes. These apes seized all the goods and gear, breaking the ship, but spared the men. Then they perceived a great house and entered it, but nobody was there. At nightfall, however, a frightful giant entered, and began to feel the men one by one, till he found the fattest, and him the giant roasted over a fire and ate like a chicken. This happened many days, till Sindbad encouraged his friends, and they heated two iron spits in the fire, and while the giant slept put out his eyes. While they ran to the shore, where they had built a raft, the giant, bellowing with rage, returned with two ghuls, and pelted the raft with rocks, killing some, but the rest escaped. However, three only were alive when they reached land.

The shore on which these three landed was occupied by an immense serpent, like a dragon, who instantly ate one of the three, while Sindbad and the other climbed up a tree. Next day the serpent glided up the tree, and ate the second. Then Sindbad descended, and with planks bound himself all round so that he was a man surrounded by a fence. Thus did he abide safe from the serpent till a ship saved him.

Now on his fourth voyage Sindbad's ship was wrecked, and he fell among hairy men, cannibals, who fattened all that they caught like cattle, and consumed them. He being thin and wasted by all his misfortunes, escaped death, and saw all his comrades fattened and roasted, till they went mad, with cries of anguish. It chanced that the shepherd, who tended these men in the folds, took pity on Sindbad and showed him the road out of danger, which taking, he arrived, after divers adventures and difficulties, at the country of a great king. In this country all were horsemen, but the saddle was unknown, so Sindbad made first the king, and afterwards the vizir, both saddle and stirrups, which so delighted them that he was advanced to great fortune and honour.

Then was he married to a maiden most beautiful and chaste, so lovely to behold that she ravished the senses, and he lived like one in a dream. But it came to pass that she died, and when they buried her they took Sindbad and shut him in the Place of the Dead with her, giving him a little food and water till he should die. Such was the custom, that husband and wife should accompany the dead wife or husband in the Place of the Dead--a mighty cave strewn with dead bodies, dark as night, and littered with jewels.

While Sindbad bewailed his lot in this place the doors opened, a dead body of a man was brought in, and with it his live wife, to whom food was given. Then Sindbad killed this fair lady with the bone of a leg, took her food and jewels, and thus did he serve all the live people thrust into the cavern. One day he heard a strange sound far up the cavern, and perceived in the distance a wild beast. Then he knew that there must be some entrance at that far end, and journeying thither, found a hole in the mountain which led to the sea. On the shore Sindbad piled all his jewels, returning every day to the cavern to gather more, till a ship came and bore him away.

His fifth voyage was interrupted by rocs, whose egg the sailors had smashed open to see the interior of what they took to be a dome.

These birds flew over the ship with rocks in their claws, and let them fall on to the ship, so that it was wrecked.

Sindbad reached shore on a plank, and wandering on this island perceived an old man, very sad, seated by a river. The old man signalled to Sindbad that he should carry him on his back to a certain point, and this Sindbad very willingly bent himself to do. But once upon his back, the legs over the shoulders and wound round about his flanks, the old man refused to get off, and drove Sindbad hither and thither with most cruel blows. At last Sindbad took a gourd, hollowed it out, filled it with grape juice, stopped the mouth, and set it in the sun. Then did he drink of this wine and get merry and forget his misery, dancing with the old man on his neck. So the old man asked for the gourd, and drank of it, and fell sleepy, and dropped from Sindbad's neck, and Sindbad slew him.

After that, Sindbad amassed treasure by pelting apes with pebbles, who threw back at him cocoanuts, which he sold for money.

On his sixth voyage Sindbad was wrecked on the most frightful mountain which no ship could pass. The sight of all the useless wealth strewn upon this terrible place of wreck and death drove all the other passengers mad, so that they died. But Sindbad, finding a stream, built a raft, and drifted with it, till, almost dead, he arrived among Indians and Abyssinians. Here he was well treated, grew rich, and returned in prosperity to Baghdad.

But once again did he travel, and this time his vessel encountered in the middle seas three vast fish-like islands, which lashed out and destroyed the ship, eating most, but Sindbad escaped. When he reached land he found himself well cared for among kind people, and he grew rich in an old man's house, who married him to his only daughter. One day after the old man's death, and when he was as rich as any in that land, lo! all the men grew into the likeness of birds, and Sindbad begged one of them to take him on his back on the mysterious flight to which they were now bent. After persuasion the man-bird agreed, and Sindbad was carried up into the firmament till he could hear the angels glorifying God in the heavenly dome. Carried away by ecstasy, he shouted praise of Allah into the holy place, and instantly the bird fell to the ground, for they were evil and incapable of praising God. But Sindbad returned to his wife, and she told him how evil were those people, and that her father was not of them, and induced him to carry her to his own land. So he sold all his possessions, took ship, and came to Baghdad, where he lived in great splendour and honour, and this was the seventh and last voyage of Sindbad the Sailor.

KARTINDO PUBLISHING HOUSE (Kartindo.com)

II.--The Tale of the Three Apples

The Caliph Haroun al-Raschid, walking by night in the city, found a fisherman lamenting that he had caught nothing for his wife and children. "Cast again," said the caliph, "and I will give thee a hundred gold pieces for whatsoever cometh up." So the man cast his net, and there came up a box, wherein was found a young damsel foully murdered. Now, to this murder confessed two men, a youth and an old man; and this was the story of the youth.

His wife fell ill, and had a longing for apples, so that he made the journey to Bussorah, and bought three apples from the caliph's gardener. But his wife would not eat them. One day, as he sat in his shop, passed a slave, bearing one of the apples. The husband asked how he came by it, whereat replied the slave that his mistress gave it him, saying that her wittol of a husband had journeyed to Bussorah for it. Then in rage the young man returned and slew his wife. Presently his little son came home, saying that he was afraid of his mother; and when the father questioned him, replied the child that he had taken one of his mother's three apples to play with, and that a slave had stolen it. Then did the husband know his wife to be innocent, and he told her father all, and they both mourned for her, and both offered themselves to the executioner--the one that he was guilty, the other to save his son-in-law whose guilt was innocence.

From this story followed that of Noureddin and his son Bedreddin Hassan, whose marriage to the Lady of Beauty was brought about by a genie, in spite of great difficulties. And it was after hearing this tale that Haroun al-Raschid declared to his vizir: "It behoves that these stories be written in letters of liquid gold."

III.--Hassan, the Rope-Maker

Two men, so it chanced, disputing whether wealth could give happiness, came before the shop of a poor rope-maker. Said one of the men: "I will give this fellow two hundred pieces of gold, and see what he does with it." Hassan, amazed by this gift, put the gold in his turban, except ten pieces, and went forth to buy hemp for his trade and meat for his children.

As he journeyed, a famished vulture made a pounce at the meat, and Hassan's turban fell off, with which the vulture, balked of the meat, flew away, far out of sight.

When the two men returned they found Hassan very unhappy, and the same who had given before gave him another two hundred pieces, which Hassan hid carefully, all but ten pieces, in a pot of bran. While he was out buying hemp, his wife exchanged the pot of bran for some scouring sand with a sandman in the street. Hassan was maddened when he came home, and beat his wife, and tore her hair, and howled like an evil spirit. When his friends returned they were amazed by his tale, but the one who had as yet given nothing now gave Hassan a lump of lead picked up in the street, saying: "Good luck shall come of homely lead, where gold profits nothing."

Hassan thought but little of the lead, and when a fisherman sent among his neighbours that night for a piece of lead wherewith to mend his nets, very willingly did Hassan part with this gift, the fisherman promising him the first fish he should catch.

When Hassan's wife cut open this fish to cook it, she found within it a large piece of glass, crystal clear, which she threw to the children for a plaything. A Jewess who entered the shop saw this piece of glass, picked it up, and offered a few pieces of money for it. Hassan's wife dared not do anything now without her husband's leave, and Hassan, being summoned, refused all the offers of the Jewess, perceiving that the piece of glass was surely a precious diamond. At last the Jewess offered a hundred thousand pieces of gold, and, as this was wealth beyond wealth, Hassan very willingly agreed to the barter.

IV.--Prince Ahmed and the Fairy

Once upon a time there was a sultan who had three sons, and all these young men loved their cousin, the fatherless and motherless Nouronnihar, who lived at their father's court.

To decide which should marry the princess the sultan bade them go forth, each a separate way, and, after a time, determined to end their travels by assembling at a certain place. "He of you who brings back from his travels the greatest of rarities," said the sultan, "he shall marry the princess, my niece." To Almighty Allah was confided the rest.

The eldest of the princes, Houssain by name, consorted with merchants in his travels, but saw nothing strange or wonderful till he encountered a man crying a piece of carpet for forty pieces of gold. "Such is the magic of this carpet," protested the man, "that he who sits himself upon it is instantly transported to whatsoever place he desires to visit, be it over wide seas or tall mountains." The prince bought this carpet, amused himself with it for some time, and then flew joyfully to the place of assembly.

Hither came the second prince, Ali, who brought from Persia an ivory tube, down which, if any man looked, he beheld the sight that most he desired to see; and the third prince, the young Ahmed, who had bought for thirty-five pieces of gold a magic apple, the smell of which would restore a soul almost passed through the gate of death.

The three princes, desiring to see their beloved princess, looked down Ali's ivory tube, and, lo! the tragic sight that met their gaze--for the princess lay at the point of death.

Swiftly did they seat themselves upon Houssain's magic carpet, and in a moment of time found themselves beside the princess, whom Ahmed instantly restored to life and beauty and health by his magic apple.

As it seemed impossible to decide which of these rare things was the rarest, the sultan commanded that each prince should shoot an arrow, and he whose arrow flew farthest should become the husband of Nouronnihar.

Houssain drew the first bow; then Ali, whose arrow sped much farther, and then Ahmed, whose arrow was not to be found.

Houssain, in despair, gave up his right of succession to the throne, and, with a blighted heart, went out into the wilderness to become a holy man. Ali was married to the princess, and Ahmed went forth into the world to seek his lost arrow.

After long wandering, Ahmed found his arrow among desolate rocks, too far for any man to have shot with the bow; and, while he looked about him, amazed and dumfounded, he beheld an iron door in the rocks, which yielded to his touch and led into a very sumptuous palace. There advanced towards him a lady of surpassing loveliness, who announced that she was a genie, that she knew well who he was, and had sent the carpet, the tube, and the apple, and had guided his arrow to her door. Furthermore, she confessed to the prince great love for him, and offered him all that she possessed, leading him to a vast and magnificent chamber, where a marriage-feast was prepared for them.

Prince Ahmed was happy for some while, and then he thought of his father, grieving for him, and at last obtained leave from the beautiful genie to go on a visit to his home. At first his father was glad to see him, but afterwards jealousy of his son and the son's secret place of dwelling, and suspicion that a son so rich and powerful might have designs on his throne, led his father to lay hard and cruel burdens on Prince Ahmed.

However, all that he commanded Ahmed performed by help of the genie, even things the most impossible. He brought a tent which would cover the sultan's army, and yet, folded up, lay in the hollow of a man's hand. This and many other wonderful things did Ahmed perform, till the sultan asked for a man one foot and a half in height, with a beard thirty feet long, who could carry a bar of iron weighing five hundredweight.

Such a man the genie found, and the sultan, beholding him, turned away in disgust; whereat the dwarf flew at him in a rage, and with his iron bar smote him to death.

Thus, too, did the little man treat all the wicked courtiers and sorcerers who had incensed the sultan against his son. And Ahmed and the genie became sultan and sultana of all that world, while Ali and Nouronnihar reigned over a great province bestowed upon them by Prince Ahmed.

As for Houssain, he forsook not the life of a holy man living in the wilderness.

V.--The Hunchback

There lived long ago a poor tailor with a pretty wife to whom he was tenderly attached. One day there came to his door a hunchback, who played upon a musical instrument and sang to it so amusingly that the tailor straightway carried him to his wife. So delighted by the hunchback's singing was the tailor's wife that she cooked a dish of fish and the three sat down to be merry. But in the midst of the feast a bone stuck in the hunchback's throat, and before a man could stare he was dead. Afraid that they should be accused of murder, the tailor conspired with his wife what they should do. "I have it," said he, and getting a piece of money he sallied forth at dark with the hunchback's body and arrived before the house of a doctor.

Here knocked he on the door, and giving the maid a piece of money, bade her hasten the doctor to his need. So soon as the maid's back was turned, he placed the hunchback on the top stair and fled. Now the doctor, coming quickly, struck against the corpse so that it fell to the bottom of the stairs. "Woe is me, for I have killed a patient!" said he, and fearing to be accused of murder, carried the body in to his wife.

Now they had a neighbour who was absent from home, and going to his room they placed the corpse against the fireplace. This man, returning and crying out: "So it is not the rats who plunder my larder!" began to belabour the hunchback, till the body rolled over and lay still. Then in great fear of his deed, this Mussulman carried the corpse into the street, and placed it upright against a shop.

Came by a Christian merchant at dawn of day, and running against the hunchback tumbled him over; then thinking himself attacked he struck the body, and at that moment the watch came by and haled the merchant before the sultan.

Now the hunchback was a favourite of the sultan, and he ordered the Christian merchant to be executed.

To the scaffold, just when death was to be done, came the Mussulman, and confessed that he was the murderer. So the executioner released the Christian, and was about to hang the other, when the doctor came and confessed to being the murderer. So the doctor took the place of the Mussulman, when the tailor and his wife hastened to the scene, and confessed that they were guilty.

Now, when this story came to the ears of the sultan, he said: "Great is Allah, whose will must be done!" and he released all of them, and commanded this story of the hunchback to be written in a book.

KARTINDO PUBLISHING HOUSE (Kartindo.com)

VI.--*Aladdin, or the Wonderful Lamp*

There was in the old time a bad and idle boy who lived with his mother, a poor widow, and gave her much unrest. And there came to him one day a wicked magician, who called himself the boy's uncle, and made rich presents to the mother, and one day he led Aladdin out to make him a merchant. Now, the magician knew by his magic of a vast hoard of wealth, together with a wonderful lamp, which lay in the earth buried in Aladdin's name. And he sent the boy to fetch the lamp, giving him a magic ring, and waited on the earth for his return. But Aladdin, his pockets full of jewels, refused to give up the lamp till his false uncle helped him to the surface of the earth, and in rage the magician caused the stone to fall upon the cave, and left Aladdin to die.

But as he wept, wringing his hands, the genie of the magic ring appeared, and by his aid Aladdin was restored to his mother. There, with the genie of the lamp to wait upon him, he lived, till, seeing the sultan's daughter pass on her way to the bath, he conceived violent love for her, and sent his mother to the sultan with all his wonderful jewels, asking the princess in marriage. The sultan, astonished by the gift of jewels, set Aladdin to perform prodigies of wonder, but all these he accomplished by aid of the genie, so that at last the sultan was obliged to give him the princess in marriage. And Aladdin caused a great pavilion to rise near the sultan's palace, and this was one of the wonders of the world, and there he abode in honour and fame.

Then the wicked magician, knowing by magic the glory of Aladdin, came disguised, crying "New Lamps for Old!" and one of the maids in the pavilion gave him the wonderful lamp, and received a new one from the coppersmith. The magician transplanted the pavilion to

Africa, and Aladdin, coming home, found the sultan enraged against him and his palace vanished. But by means of the genie of the ring he discovered the whereabouts of his pavilion, and going thither, slew the magician, possessed himself anew of the lamp, and restored his pavilion to its former site.

But the magician's wicked brother, plotting revenge, obtained access to the princess in disguise of a holy woman he had foully murdered, and he would have certainly slain Aladdin but for a warning of the genie, by which Aladdin was enabled to kill the magician. After that Aladdin lived in glory and peace, and ascended in due course to the throne, and reigned with honour and mercy.

KARTINDO PUBLISHING HOUSE (Kartindo.com)

VII.--Ali Baba and the Forty Thieves

Now, the father of Ali Baba left both his sons poor; but Kasim married a rich wife, and so he lived plenteously, while his poor brother, Ali Baba, worked in the wood. It came to pass that Ali Baba one day saw in the wood a company of forty robbers, the captain of whom cried, "Open, Sesame!" to a great rock, and lo! it opened, and the men disappeared. When they were gone out again, Ali Baba came from his hiding, and, addressing the rock in the same way, found that it obeyed him. Then went he in and took much of the treasure, which he drove home on his mule. Now, when his wife sent to the brother Kasim for scales, wherewith she might weigh all this treasure, the sister-in-law being suspicious that one so poor should have need of scales, smeared the bottom of the pan with wax and grease, and discovered on the return a gold piece. This she showed to Kasim, who made Ali Baba confess the tale. Then Kasim went to the cave, entered, loaded much treasure, and was about to depart, when he found he had forgotten the magic words whereby he entered. There was he found by the forty thieves, who slew and quartered him. Ali Baba found the quarters, took them home, got a blind tailor to sew them together, and gave his brother burial.

Now, the robbers discovered Ali Baba's house, and they hid themselves in oil-jars hung on the backs of mules, and the captain drove them. Thus came they to Ali Baba's house, and the captain craved lodging for himself and his beasts. Surely would Ali Baba have been captured, tortured, and put to death but for his maid, the faithful and astute Morgiana, who discovered men in the jars, and, boiling cans of oil, poured it upon them one by one, and so delivered her master. But the captain had escaped, and Ali Baba still went in great fear of his life. But when he returned, disguised so that he might have puzzled the wisest, Morgiana recognised the enemy of her master; and she was dancing before him and filling his eyes with pleasure; and when it came for her to take the tambourine and go round for largess, she strengthened her heart and, quick as the blinding lightning, plunged a dagger into his vitals. Thus did the faithful Morgiana save her master, and he married her to his nephew, the son of Kasim, and they lived long in great joy and blessing.

KARTINDO PUBLISHING HOUSE (Kartindo.com)

VIII.--The Fisherman and the Genie

There was once a poor fisherman who every day cast his net four times into the sea. On a day he went forth, and casting in his net, drew up with great labour a dead jackass; casting again, an earthen pitcher full of sand; casting a third time vexatiously, potsherds and shattered glass; and at the last a jar of yellow copper, leaden-capped, and stamped with the seal-ring of Solomon, the son of David. His rage was silenced at sight of the sacred seal, and, removing the cap, smoke issued, which, taking vast shape, became a terrible genie frightful to see.

Said the genie: "By what manner of death wilt thou die, for I have sworn, by Allah, to slay the man who freed me!" He moreover explained how Solomon had placed him in the jar for heresy, and how he had lain all those years at the bottom of the sea. For a hundred years, he said, he swore that he would make rich for ever and ever the man who freed him; for the next hundred, that for such an one he would open the hoards of the earth; then, that he would perfectly fulfil such an one's three wishes; finally, in his rage, that he would kill the man who freed him.

Now, the fisherman, having pleaded in vain, said that he did not believe the tale, seeing that so huge a genie could never have got into so small a jar. Whereat the genie made smoke of himself, and re-entered the vase. Instantly then did the fisherman stopper it, nor would he let the genie free till that wicked one had promised to spare his life and do him service. Grudgingly and wrathfully did the genie issue forth, but being now under oath to Allah, he spared the fisherman and did him service.

KARTINDO PUBLISHING HOUSE (Kartindo.com)

He took him to a lake in the black mountains, bade him throw in his net, and bear the catch to the sultan. Now, by the fisherman's catching of four fish all of a different hue, the sultan discovered that this lake in the mountains was once a populous and mighty city, whereof the prince and all the inhabitants had been bewitched in ancient time. When the city was restored and all those many people called back to life, the sultan enriched the fisherman, who lived afterwards in wealth.

KARTINDO PUBLISHING HOUSE (Kartindo.com)

IX.--The Enchanted Horse

In olden times there came to the Court of Persia a stranger from Ind, riding a horse made of wood, which, said he, could fly whithersoever its rider wished. When the sultan had seen the horse fly to a mountain and back, he asked the Hindu its price, and said the man: "Thy daughter's hand." Now the prince, standing by, was enraged at this insolence, but his father said: "Have no fear that I should do this thing. Howsoever, lest another king become possessed of the horse, I will bargain for it." But the impetuous prince, doubting the truth of the horse's power, jumped upon its back, turned the peg which he had observed the Hindu to turn, and instantly was borne far away.

The king, enraged that the Hindu could not bring back his son, had the man cast into prison, albeit the Hindu protested that soon the prince must discover the secret of stopping the horse by means of a second peg, and therefore would soon return.

Now the prince did not discover this secret till he was far away, and it was night. He came to earth near a palace, and going in, found there an exquisite lady sleeping, and knew by her dress that she was of a rank equal with his own. Then he pleaded to her for succour, and she constrained him to stay, and for many weeks he abode as a guest. After that time he said, "Come to my father's court, that we may be married!" And early one dawn he bore her to Persia on the back of the enchanted horse.

So glad was the king at his son's return that he released the Hindu.

Now the Hindu, hearing what had happened, determined on revenge. He found where the horse was placed, and going to the palace where the foreign princess was housed, sent for her in the sultan's name, and she came to him. Then he seated her upon the horse, and mounting up in full view of the sultan and his royal son, flew far away with his lovely captive.

It was the Hindu's desire to marry this princess, but when they were come to earth, she withstood him, and cried for help and succour. To her came the sultan of that place, and slew the Hindu, and would have married her, but she was faithful to her lover and feigned madness.

Then the sultan offered rewards to any who should cure her of this frightful madness, and many physicians came and failed. Now, her lover, distracted at sight of seeing her in mid-air with the Hindu, had turned Holy Man, roaming the earth without hope like one who is doomed.

It happened that he came to the palace where the princess lay in her feigned madness, and hearing the tale of her, and of the enchanted horse, with new hope and a great joy in his heart, he went in, disguised as a physician, and in secret made himself known.

Then he stood before the sultan of that land, and said: "From the enchanted horse hath she contracted this madness, and by the enchanted horse shall she lose it." And he gave orders to dress her in glorious array, to crown her with jewels and gold, and to lead her forth to the palace square.

A vast concourse assembled there, and the prince set his beloved lady on the horse, and pretending incantations, leapt suddenly upon its back, turned the peg, and as the enchanted steed flew towards Persia, over his shoulder cried the glad prince: "When next, O sultan, thou wouldst marry a princess who implores thy protection, ask first for her consent."

The End

KARTINDO PUBLISHING HOUSE (Kartindo.com)